T0209443

As You're Going

Practical Discipleship for Practical People

BRETT HARIG

WESTBOW
PRESS®
A DIVISION OF THOMAS NELSON
& ZONDERVAN

WestBow Press books may be ordered through booksellers or by contacting:

WestBow Press
A Division of Thomas Nelson & Zondervan
1663 Liberty Drive
Bloomington, IN 47403
www.westbowpress.com
1 (866) 928-1240

ISBN: 978-1-9736-3559-8 (sc)
ISBN: 978-1-9736-3558-1 (hc)
ISBN: 978-1-9736-3560-4 (e)

Library of Congress Control Number: 2018909075

Print information available on the last page.

WestBow Press rev. date: 08/03/2018

Dedication

To new disciples of Jesus Christ.

Acknowledgments

I thank my wonderful wife, Becky, my son, Will, and my yet-to-be-born Summer Grace. I love you all so much.

I thank Brian and Kyle for keeping me on the right path, and I thank Gene and Josh for accountability and growth.

Contents

Introduction

A friend of mine asked me to speak to a group one night. I started with a few simple questions to get started. "How many of you are saved?" All but one hand went up in the group of ten to fifteen people. "All right, cool. So how many of you have been saved for a year or less?" One hand went up. "How many have been saved for five years or less?" Two or three more hands went up. "How many have been saved for ten years or less?" All the rest of the hands went up in the room. "So when you got saved, how many of you had someone tell you, 'Congratulations and welcome to the kingdom of heaven! Now let me show you and help you out on your new walk with God and learn what He expects of you'?" No one raised a hand.

That is the biggest problem I see with the church today—few people if any are discipling others.

What I do matters? Yes, it has an earthly impact, but more important, it has an eternal impact on God's kingdom. All God's children are building His kingdom, not just those who are known worldwide or are in the media or on television. Every single one of us makes an impact. So will you be a part of a greater impact for God's kingdom or do nothing and make it harder for everyone else?

CHAPTER 1

Discipleship

Have you ever reached a place in your Christian walk that you didn't know where to go from there? I think every Christian has experienced that at some time or another. Some say, "I'm not sure what I'm supposed to be doing right now" or "I just don't know what to do."

At that time in my life, I thought I had been growing spiritually, but I just kind of hit a wall and didn't know where to go from there. I prayed and asked God to give me direction on where He wanted me to go. I got an answer, and it was the last thing I expected.

A New Start

My pastor and I usually take turns leading our men's group on a four- to six-week rotation. God showed me part of what I was to do next with my life about halfway through my pastor's rotation. The word *discipleship* would not leave my mind. Imagine listening to your favorite album or CD for hours on repeat, but all it said was "Discipleship." That's what was going through my mind.

I looked for some material for this discipleship lesson I didn't know how to prepare for. I couldn't find anything that really expressed what was on my heart. Then I heard the Lord tell me, "Write it." Imagine me, a guy who never cared anything for language arts or reading or expository writing in school thinking I was going to write the material for this study. Nope! Not going to happen. But it did.

I started asking myself about discipleship, and writing down what I came up with opened my mind to a lot of things I'd never thought of before or had put much thought into. But never did I think this short study of eight or nine pages would turn into something like this.

What Is It?

What is a disciple? One dictionary describes a disciple as "someone who follows another person or another way of life and who submits him/herself to the discipline (teaching) of that leader or way."

So let's break down the word. *Disciple* comes from the koine Greek word *mathetes*, which means a pupil or an apprentice to a master craftsman. The Latin word *discipulus,* which means learner, leads to the English definition of student. So when you look at where the word *disciple* comes from, there is always a student and teacher or apprentice and master. In the case of being disciples for Christ, we are always the student or apprentice and Christ is always the teacher or the master.

The next question that popped into my head was, *Am I a disciple?* Well, the answer may be hard to answer. Am I sold out to Jesus and His ministry and want to learn and mimic everything there is to know about Him? Or do I fake it on Sundays and do whatever I want every other day? I can't be a follower on Sunday and a fan throughout the rest of the week; I must be a follower every day.

So if we are followers and not fans of Jesus as Christians, are we disciples? Yes should be your answer if you are truly following Christ. We are all called to be His disciples.

Qualifications

Many things run through my mind when I think of disciples, for example, handpicked by Jesus, hung out with Jesus in the flesh, and able to perform miracles in Jesus's name. Then I think about how I have nothing in common with these characteristics.

The enemy wants you to think you're not good enough to be a disciple for Jesus. You doubt, you fear, you know better, you don't know the Word well enough— so on and so on. But take a look at the disciples. They did the same things I fail at daily, yet He called them to be disciples.

Luke gave a few qualifications for becoming a disciple of Jesus. A large crowd was following Jesus. He said to them,

> If you want to be my disciple, you must, by comparison, hate everyone else—your father and mother, wife and children,

brothers and sisters—yes, even your own life. Otherwise, you cannot be my disciple. And if you do not carry your own cross and follow me, you cannot be my disciple.

But don't begin until you count the cost. For who would begin construction of a building without first calculating the cost to see if there is enough money to finish it? Otherwise, you might complete only the foundation before running out of money, and then everyone would laugh at you. They would say, "There's the person who started that building and couldn't afford to finish it!"

Or what king would go to war against another king without first sitting down with his counselors to discuss whether his army of 10,000 could defeat the 20,000 soldiers marching against him? And if he can't, he will send a delegation to discuss terms of peace while the enemy is still far away. So you cannot become my disciple without giving up everything you own. (Luke 14:25–33 NLT)

We must be sold out to Jesus. Our love for Him has to surpass that for everything in our lives—our families, children, parents, and even ourselves. If we believe Jesus is the Son of God who came to save us from lives of sin and we want the Lord's will to be done in all aspects of our lives and live selflessly for Him, we qualify.

Slumped Life

A few years ago, I was in a slump in my life and didn't know where to go. I had lost a job that let me be off every Sunday and landed one that required my working most weekends. At the time, I didn't realize that most of my prayer, reading, and fellowship took place on only one day. I was disconnected from God. Through my doing, not His, I had distanced myself from Him.

I play in a Christian band, and we usually meet weekly. Many times over the next few years, that was the only spiritual thing I took part in. At the time, it was because I loved to play music. I got caught up in the world. I let my new job run my schedule and new coworkers lead me astray. I found myself gradually further and further from where God had called me to be. I had become part of a movement in our society recognized as cultural Christianity. I was a Christian, but I didn't walk in the faith or even recognize it. I knew what it was to be a Christian, but I kept to only what I thought was biblical.

Back to the band. We would fellowship, experience

some spiritual learning if we were writing a new song, and have music and prayer at the end. I was going through the motions. I was there just because it was fun to play music. I didn't realize at the time that the two guys I spent the most time with, Brian and Kyle, were holding onto my spiritual lifeline and didn't know it. I didn't know that either. I had a family to be a part of and at least try to help raise my son and be a husband, but I didn't know what to do.

But even in my slump, God had a plan for me. This was the start of something pretty amazing. The band, composed of three very different people, rekindled my love for Christ. God built us into brothers. Our small group sparked it for me. I needed their guidance, conversation, and fellowship. It was my church service. They were and still are training me as a disciple. That has changed my life.

Then one time at work, a bold, out-of-the-box Christian guy started asking me about God and Jesus. That was the forbidden thing to do in our society; you don't talk about religion at work because that's against all human resources and social policies. The thing about it, though, was that he wasn't talking about religion; he was talking about a relationship. This guy was my church service at work—nothing but encouragement, uplifting conversation, and leadership counsel.

These people helped me when I was a Christian but wasn't feeling any personal connection with God. At such times, however, God puts people in your life for a season. They may leave after that, but while they're there, they can have a huge impact.

Discipleship can be like what I experienced; it can occur in a small-group setting or one on one. It helped me get out of my state of mind. They were training and teaching me to better my walk with Christ whether they knew it or not.

When I was younger, I had Christian friends who never brought that up unless they were asked about it. I'm at the point in my life that I want anyone who comes in contact with me to see Jesus, the Gospels, and the good news of Jesus. I don't want to be the backdoor Christian who talks about Jesus only when no one is looking. I want everyone to see Him in me. On countless times with the band, I've missed out on blessings and made others miss out because my mind and pride were on me rather than on the Lord. I'm not going to miss those opportunities anymore because of my flesh.

Non-Discipleship

Non-discipleship, I believe, is the worst epidemic to ever happen to the church. When I, you, Christians— the church—decide not to make disciples, we are doing more harm than anything else. Who are we training to lead the next generation and for missions all over the world? We are setting the next generation up for failure because we aren't doing our jobs. We are all called as Christians to be disciples.

In Matthew 28, Jesus gave us the Great Commission: "Go and make disciples of all nations." A lot of us think Jesus was speaking to those of us who are called to go, not us. This is the mind-set the world wants us to have so we won't actually make disciples. Just think: if Jesus could turn the world upside down with eleven men—Judas was dead at that time—what can God do through us if we all disciple just one person? I'm sure there would be more than eleven. And then what if they discipled one person each? There would be an uprising of Christians ready to change the world.

Guidance

I've often had conversations with people about what the church does for them, and it's sad to hear and see how little the church is doing these days. I can't stand to hear about new Christians struggling due to a lack of guidance. Christians think that when nonbelievers visit a church, they know everything there is to know about God and the Bible. If that were the case, we'd all have the ultimate knowledge and wouldn't need anything or anyone. That's not the case at all. It's up to us as Christians to help them on their journeys. Nonbelievers don't know any better because they haven't been taught any better. We can't expect them to come into service and act like Christians when they don't know what it is to be a Christian.

Throughout this book, we'll discuss what we are called to do—disciple others and help them and ourselves in our walk with Christ.

How do we become better disciples? Let's start by considering what we're called to do; we must learn about Jesus and His ministry.

CHAPTER 2

Learn and Teach

Reading the Bible is not just reading a book; it's reading the real, living breath of God. Every word was dictated by the Holy Spirit to man. It's reading the words of God and getting to know Him and His character. It's the basis of building a relationship with Him.

Daily Chores

I read a book recently in which the author described a time in his life when he was disconnected from God and was just going through the motions. He described his daily devotion and study time as a regular chore: "It's boring. I don't understand it. It's too hard." And yet he realized that to learn about God and His character, he was supposed to read and study His Word.

If it's a relationship with God we're looking for, He's already there; we just have to discover Him. I wouldn't come home from work and pay no attention to my wife—especially if the lights were down, a couple of candles were lit, and the kids were at Grandma's. I wouldn't tell her I wasn't interested and ignore her. We wouldn't treat our spouses like that, would we? That would be very insulting to them and everything they've done to make that happen. Do we treat God that way? How do you think He feels when He's put forth all this effort and we ignore Him and walk way?

It's not just a daily chore; it's building a relationship. We first have to learn ourselves before we can start discipling others. Daily reading and devotions, small groups, and worship services are all ways to learn about God—who He is and what He expects of us. We can start discipling others only when we grow and learn about Him, ourselves.

You Know What You Know

What's your favorite book or story in the Bible? How well do you know it? As in really knowing it like the back of your hand? Could you tell it backward? Tell someone else about it? Teach them about it? You'll see how good you know it and how easy it is to teach when you're really comfortable with the material. It's like showing someone how to use a machine you've used for ten years. You know it; you know how it slightly changes when you adjust pressure knob number 2, or how often that belt needs to be changed down to the second, or how an imperfection will occur at 1.15 plus or minus RMS over or under the given specifications. We are called to teach the Word like that to others.

Being Led by the Spirit

We must remember when reading for ourselves and teaching others to let the Holy Spirit lead us. This is a big part we miss the mark on a lot. Only with His guidance can we follow Him correctly. We forget about the Holy Spirit, or at least I do or did.

I grew up in a Southern Baptist church for the majority of my childhood. I had heard the Holy Spirit mentioned but never knew what His job was in my life. Back then, my best friend's dad was a pastor. I'm grateful to him for setting me up with a foundation of the gospel. I went to church with them Wednesday nights, Sunday mornings, and Sunday nights. I was there when the church doors were unlocked. At that time, my parents didn't go to church or went to a different church.

The first time I went with my parents to church, a woman in the back row—I later found out she was the pastor's mother—stood and raised her hands during a very emotional altar call. Out of her mouth came words I didn't understand. As she was speaking, the pastor was very emotionally speaking phrases or words as soon as they left her mouth. Later on, I realized that he was interpreting the words the woman was speaking. At the same time as I was questioning what was going on, I felt a sense of peace throughout the church. I remember it to this day almost twenty years later. I was kind of scared of it, but it raised questions that I kept in mind for almost twenty years. I didn't want to know or want to experience that again.

While I was studying one day, I was reading about spiritual gifts, the difference between them, and how they worked. Speaking in tongues is one. That gift is not everyone's, but we can't dismiss it. This is where discernment comes in; we have to make sure that number one, it's from God. That is how the Holy Spirit works. We have to let Him lead us in what we do. Jesus didn't send the Holy Spirit here just for a short time after He was resurrected; the Holy Spirit is here with us today, and we need to let Him lead.

In a sense, spiritual gifts have to do with learning and teaching. When we let the Spirit lead us, we will realize what our spiritual gifts are. We are to use them for His sake and for the benefit the body of Christ. When we read and learn about God and His character, the Holy Spirit gives us guidance and insight as to what our path is and what His will is for us. Knowing who the Holy Spirit is- is crucial in our walk with Christ.

The Holy Spirit is not an it or a thing; He is a member of the Trinity and wants a relationship with us. John 14:26 (NLT) describes the Holy Spirit: "But when the Father sends the Advocate as my representative—that is, the Holy Spirit—he will teach you everything and will remind you of everything I have told you."

Power of the Spirit

Knowing that we can't change anything, that only God can change us through the Holy Spirit is key. Whatever I do is from Him. Whatever I teach is from

Him. Whatever I write is from Him. Nothing is from me, and nothing benefits me—it's all glory to God.

The power of the Holy Spirit is indescribable. We have to remember that the Spirit we have today is the same Spirit who was here when Jesus walked the earth and even before that. Let's take Saul for example. We know that he hunted down Christians. He was present at the execution of Stephen, the first martyr: "Then they cast him out of the city and stoned him. And the witnesses laid down their garments at the feet of a young man named Saul."

Saul did everything he could to stop the movement of Christ throughout the land until Saul met the Lord on the way to Damascus and was changed. His character was changed, his heart was changed, and his mind was changed. His encounter with Jesus filled him with the Holy Spirit and drastically altered his life.

God changed the names of Abram and his wife, Sarai, to Abraham and Sarah. I know it doesn't seem like a big deal or much of a change, but in their culture, what your name meant was important. Abram meant high father or exalted father; not too bad for a name's meaning, but the Lord told him he would father a nation, and He changed his name to Abraham, meaning the father of many nations (Genesis 17:1–5).

The same thing with Sarai, whose name meant my lady or my princess; Sarah meant the mother of many nations (Genesis 17:15–16). The power of God and His Spirit are so great that none can compare to it. It's through Him alone that we can change plain and simple—not through us but through God.

Setting a Foundation

Reading and learning the Word is the foundation of our faith in Jesus. The most common way to view that foundation is to consider the strongest beam, brick, or concrete that supports the rest of a structure. The Word is a firm foundation we can stand strong on in times of trouble, need, and questioning.

Jesus talked about a man who sowed seeds.

> Later that same day Jesus left the house and sat beside the lake. A large crowd soon gathered around him, so he got into a boat. Then he sat there and taught as the people stood on the shore. He told many stories in the form of parables, such as this one:
>
> "Listen! A farmer went out to plant some seeds. As he scattered them across his field, some seeds fell on a footpath, and the birds came and ate them. Other seeds fell on shallow soil with underlying rock. The seeds sprouted quickly because the soil was shallow. But the plants soon

wilted under the hot sun, and since they didn't have deep roots, they died. Other seeds fell among thorns that grew up and choked out the tender plants. Still other seeds fell on fertile soil, and they produced a crop that was thirty, sixty, and even a hundred times as much as had been planted!" (Matthew 13:1–8 NLT)

"Now listen to the explanation of the parable about the farmer planting seeds: The seed that fell on the footpath represents those who hear the message about the Kingdom and don't understand it. Then the evil one comes and snatches away the seed that was planted in their hearts. The seed on the rocky soil represents those who hear the message and immediately receive it with joy. But since they don't have deep roots, they don't last long. They fall away as soon as they have problems or are persecuted for believing God's word. The seed that fell among the thorns represents those who hear God's word, but all too quickly the message is crowded out by the worries of this life and the lure of wealth, so no fruit is produced. The seed that fell on good soil represents those who truly hear and understand God's word and produce a harvest of thirty, sixty, or even a hundred times as much as had been planted!" (Matthew 13:18–23 NLT)

What foundation do you have? Are you on the path that has no roots at all and can be carried away as though you had never heard the gospel? Are you on the rocky ground where you've heard the Word and think you're ready to go out when your roots have not grasped anything and your fire has gone out before you knew it?

The thorns are a little tricky because you've heard the Word and have taken root in it, but the first time someone questions your faith, you lose all spark and have no roots.

Good soil? That's where you know the Word, are firmly settled in it, and are ready to change the world.

You cannot plant seeds in good soil if you're not there yourself. How can you plant seeds in good soil from the path, the rocks, or the thorns? You can't, but God can. God's Word never returns void; it always turns for the good. If we are not firmly rooted in the Word, we may be hurting more than helping others. Being led by the Spirit is so important; we have to be sure that when we are reading, speaking, or teaching the Word, we are following Him and not jumping ahead of ourselves when we aren't ready.

The Closet

But when you pray, go away by yourself, shut the door behind you, and pray to your Father in private. Then your Father, who sees everything, will reward you. (Matthew 6:6 NLT)

Find your closet, prayer room, or place where you find freedom, a secret place for you and God to spend time together, just you and He. He wants to have this time with you.

I think the biggest reason we need a prayer closet is to make sure we aren't being distracted by anything while we're praying to God. We can go in, shut the door, and it's just us and God.

Maybe the next reason is to make sure that this room has purpose; we know that when we go in, it's time to pray and pray hard. It's private. Everyone in our homes should know what this room is used for; when the door is shut, they know not to enter. They know to give you privacy during your prayer time. And the last reason to have a prayer room is because Jesus said to. Red-letter Bibles have Matthew 6:6 all in red; He's helping you in your connection with God. Like I said earlier, He wants to have this time with you and longs for it. He wants this relationship with you more than you can imagine.

Biblical vs. Worldly

What the Bible says about what we should be and what the world says we should be are completely different. This is a key point Christians have to learn.

You find out what is of the world and what is of God by asking yourself one question: "What does the Bible say about it?" Use scripture to make clear what is right. Don't rely on the world to give you an answer because it will be wrong. Rely on the truth of the Bible to lead you as you grow and learn about God and His character.

What does the Bible say we are? "So God created human beings in his own image. In the image of God he created them; male and female he created them" (Genesis 1:27 NLT). We have to look into what God and His character look like.

Does God have an image of anxiety, sorrow, misery, depression, addiction, and other negative things? No. So when you or anyone you know is going through tough times with issues such as these, remember or remind them of the truth that these issues are not from God and are not what He wants us to be. These are just some of the issues He dealt with on the cross. We have to know what is from the world and what is from God.

What Does the Bible Say about Learning and Teaching?

In 2 Timothy 3:16 (NIV), we read, "All Scripture is God-breathed and is useful for teaching, rebuking, correcting and training in righteousness." That means that if we are teaching scripture, it will profit God.

Matthew 28:19–20 (NIV) reads,

> Therefore go and make disciples of all nations, baptizing them in the name of the Father and of the Son and of the Holy Spirit, and teaching them to obey everything I have commanded you And surely I am with you always, to the very end of the age.

One of the best descriptions of how discipleship works.

1 Peter 4:10 (NIV) tells us to use our spiritual gifts to help each other: "Each of you should use whatever gift you have received to serve others, as faithful stewards of God's grace in its various forms."

Acts 18:11 (NIV): "So Paul stayed in Corinth for a year and a half, teaching them the word of God."

It's not something that happens overnight; you don't just read a verse or a chapter and become an expert. It takes time. You don't meet someone today and get married tomorrow; you build a relationship first and get to know that person. It's the same with learning God's Word—you take the time to read, pray, talk with others, and worship.

Start with you first—learn about, take in, and grow with the Lord. Then give it all away—don't hoard it. It's the gift worth giving. Teaching others about the Lord to save them from an eternity in hell is the worthiest gift you could give them.

In the simplest terms, being a disciple means being a student; you need to spend your life learning from and about the Master in relationship and modeling that relationship for the whole world to see.

Prayer

Let's end this segment on "Learn and Teach" with a prayer.

God, thank you for opening my eyes to see what you have called me to do. I want to be the vessel you've called me to be and better your kingdom. I want your will to be done in my life so I can be on your path.

I ask that you prepare not only my heart for this mission but also the hearts of the people I will meet. I ask that the Holy Spirit guide me on what to learn and what to teach. Have your will and way with this servant of yours. Thank you for who you are. In Jesus's name, amen.

Correction and Accountability

Action Part I

Discipleship has different aspects of learning just as any form of learning does. I have a unique learning style just as you have yours. I have a three-part learning process. I have to hear something, read it, and write it down. It's not in a photographic way as some people have, but it's close to it if I do all these things.

This is the same with discipleship— we have to learn it, teach it, and put it into action. The action can vary on how it's presented. That's what we'll cover in this section, the first part of action.

Acceptance

We have to keep in mind a few things when we start to build our relationship with God. First, we have to make sure we accept people for who they are.

I heard a story about a church that had just gotten a new pastor. The first Sunday he came to preach, he was unrecognizable. He came dressed as a homeless man and walked around greeting everyone. He received many dirty looks; none of the congregants asked him how he was doing or if he needed some help. He sat alone in the back row.

The service started. A deacons addressed the congregation and told them about their new pastor; he eventually invited him to join him on stage. Everyone looked around waiting for the new pastor to identify himself; they saw the homeless man stand and walk toward the stage. The church was silent. The homeless man took the stage. He removed his beard. He basically said the church had a lot to work on.

How many times do we treat others this way? It's something we have to work on. Like really work on. I was guilty of it too—watching an unchurched person come into church and not doing what I should have done. It happened when I saw someone who didn't talk the way I talked or dressed the way I dressed. I was condemning them before I met them. Instant judgment. I had completely forgotten that I had been there too before.

We have to keep in mind that unchurched people don't know any different; that's what we talked about in chapter 1 in this book, "Learn and Teach." And the teaching is not from you. You didn't do anything. It was God working through you with His Holy Spirit. Only God can change people's hearts, minds, and characters.

We have to accept people for who they are and let the Spirit lead us while we are teaching and discipling them. When they learn about God—who He is and what He looks like—that will transform their lives just as ours were when we first experienced God.

Build It Up

As you learn about God—who He is and what His character is—you're building a relationship with Him. When you read the Bible, you are reading words He spoke. When you pray, you are in a deep conversation with Him. When you worship, you are praising the God who created you, me—the whole universe—and are connected with Him.

In all these ways, you build a relationship with Him, and as you do that, you ask yourself, *How can I live without failing Him?* The truth is that you can't because we are all sinners (Romans 3:23). So when we do fail, we will have the feeling that the Holy Spirit is there to correct us, and we will think, *I shouldn't have done or said that.* That's conviction. The Holy Spirit convicts us because we sinned and we know it. But He does that only out of love.

Condemnation

Condemnation is to cause someone to suffer or live in difficult or unpleasant conditions. Do you think God wants you to suffer, for any reason? The answer is no, not for any reason. He loves you. He wants a relationship with you. He sent His Son to atone for your sins, and He doesn't want you to leave earth without knowing Jesus is your Lord and Savior.

God doesn't want you to feel suffering, regret, or shame; that's what the enemy wants you to feel—that you're not good enough to have a relationship with the Lord. The enemy wants you to feel so alone and disconnected that you actually believe it. God will not cause a feeling of condemnation about who you are because He offers grace and forgiveness through His Son, Jesus Christ. Paul described condemnation as worldly grief in 2 Corinthians 7:10 (NIV): "Godly sorrow brings repentance that leads to salvation and leaves no regret, but worldly sorrow brings death."

If God had wanted you to die and live for eternity in hell, He would have just sent you there from the time you were born and you'd never have a relationship with Him. For that matter, He wouldn't have sacrificed His Son for the sins of the world. But He did. He gave you this life to believe in His Son to save you from eternal hell without God. He doesn't condemn you for how you have lived or what you've done; the enemy does that to confuse you. Such negative thoughts do not come from God. He sent His Spirit to the earth to help you overcome your sins, not to condemn you for them.

Conviction

In this section, we'll discuss the difference between conviction and condemnation. Conviction comes from the Holy Spirit. I believe that when conviction occurs, we see ourselves as God sees us. The difference between conviction and condemnation occurs here. As we discussed just a moment ago, the world condemns us here and makes us feel unwanted, but the Holy Spirit lets us see our need for forgiveness that doesn't condemn us for what we have done or how we used to be. Forgiveness leads to confession, repentance, and a cleansing of our sins.

> If we confess our sins, he is faithful and just and will forgive us our sins and purify us from all unrighteousness. (1 John 1:9 NIV)

> Repent, then, and turn to God, so that your sins may be wiped out, that times of refreshing may come from the Lord. (Acts 3:19 NIV)

> But if we walk in the light, as he is in the light, we have fellowship with one another, and the blood of Jesus, his Son, purifies us from all sin. (1 John 1:7 NIV)

Confession is exactly what it sounds like—realizing from your conviction that you have sinned and need forgiveness and confessing your sins to God.

Repentance is turning from your sin. After confessing your sins to God, you realize your sins and turn from them.

Cleansing is knowing that God has no record of your sin. To Him, it never existed.

Conviction vs. Condemnation

After considering the differences between conviction and condemnation, we should look into the matter of nonbelievers and condemnation. Let's look at what the Bible says about this.

Where Does This Fit in Here?

If you haven't questioned the placement of this section in this book as I did at first, let's consider it something we need to learn, teach, and then model. (We'll get to modeling shortly.)

Condemnation and conviction fit in here because this is where it is vital to correcting our brothers and sisters. If we don't have a strong relationship with those we are discipling or helping hold accountable, we will fail. Building our relationship with them is key to helping them. If we don't have a relationship with them, even though we are trying to help them out of love, they won't see it that way. They'll see it as an attack and think we are condemning them though that's not what we're trying to do. It's so important to be led by the Spirit to have these conversations.

Onto the next reason these subjects are in this

section—repentance. As we just covered, repentance is turning from sin that has a stronghold on us especially sin we have dealt with for a long time and find it hard to simply turn away from. It's been a lifestyle for so long or a mind-set we can't overcome.

Maybe it's just me, but maybe not. I know concerning the stronghold sins in my life, I kind of wanted to keep just a little bit of it; I thought, *Hey, it's not that bad —I could be doing worse.* So even though I knew I was sinning, my pride told me it wasn't that bad. I confessed my sins, but my pride kept me from being freed from it. I couldn't get why God wouldn't take this away from me after I confessed it, but that was because my heart wasn't right, and it took talking with my accountability group for me to realize that.

Once I talked about my sin to my accountability group and brought them into the light, the enemy's foothold over me in that area was gone. It may seem like something that you're not comfortable with at first, but once your pride gets out of the way and you start talking about your sins, you'll feel relieved because you'll know the Lord is working on you. And you'll grow exponentially closer to Him.

Weary about doing something like this? Read this scripture, pray on it, and ask God through His Spirit to reveal to you what it means.

Take no part in the worthless deeds of evil
and darkness; instead, expose them. It is
shameful even to talk about the things
that ungodly people do in secret. But their
evil intentions will be exposed when the
light shines on them, for the light makes
everything visible. This is why it is said,
"Awake, O sleeper, rise up from the dead,
and Christ will give you light." (Ephesians
5:11–14 NLT)

Fellowship

Just as is the case with our relationship with God,
we build relationships with our brothers and sisters in
Christ. Together, we learn and grow spiritually; that's
what God has called us to do. We're not supposed to do
this on our own. If we single ourselves out and don't
have any contact with others, our minds will wander,
and they can wander pretty far. We'll have no one to ask
questions to, bounce stuff off, or just talk and fellowship
with. We aren't here to do this alone because we can't
do this alone.

Arms of Mercy, the band I play in, went on a
multistate tour for a few weeks. It was the biggest move
we'd made as a band. We left our wives and children
for days at a time, something we hadn't done before.

Traveling together, on the road, just the three of us. Well, at least that's what we'd planned ...

When we got the dates for our performances on that tour, we realized that Brian, our drummer, would be out of the country for most of our gigs. *What are we going to do?* ran through our minds. It was just the three of us. Canceling our tour dates was not an option at that point because we felt God was calling us to go. We needed a drummer.

This is how God worked in our lives, and I'm glad I witnessed it firsthand. We contacted a few people we thought might be interested in going and thought we had someone locked in, but that fell through. We had someone else in mind; we talked him, and he was in. Just like that, God placed Anthony at the right time with us, and it turned out that it was the right time for him as well.

We had known him for a few years and had played a few shows with his other band. When I first met him, he wasn't very talkative and pretty much kept to himself, but over the next few weeks, I saw him transform. He opened up a little more and more each time we practiced. I saw a spark.

Our first show went better than we'd expected; no one knew he wasn't our regular drummer. The fellowship and company of all the other Christian artists let his spark get bigger and bigger. I have never seen him smile, talk, and cut up as I did while we were on tour. I realized this tour wasn't about us at all; I came to the conclusion that we were on tour to help him with his spark.

We had a blast and became closer with all the artists who were with us, and I want to thank them for being obedient. In a nutshell, we were coals set in a stove and had caught on fire—for God. We fellowshipped with other Christians, built relationships, and grew spiritually.

Though Anthony played drums for us for only a short time, he became a brother. I told him afterward that I didn't want him—I meant his coal—to get cold and lose its spark. I wanted to do whatever I could to help him with his walk with the Lord.

That's the illustration I use to describe fellowship—coals in a fire will stay on fire until they're taken out of the fire. They'll stay warm for a bit, but they'll get cold if they're not in the company of other coals. Fellowship is a very important part of our relationship with other Christians.

How to Bear It

Bear one another's burdens, He said. Galatians 6:2 (NLT) reads, "Share each other's burdens, and in this way obey the law of Christ." We are called to do this for one another. But let's back up to verse 1 of Galatians 6 (NLT): "Brothers and sisters, if someone is caught in a sin, you who live by the Spirit should restore that person gently. But watch yourselves, or you also may be tempted."

That's the hard part especially in today's society. We think, *I can't say anything about the way so-and-so acts or does this or that.* I'm sure you've filled out job applications that asked questions in a multitude of ways, but you had only one answer to them all. If you saw someone you were working with who was taking supplies home for personal use, stealing from the company, so on and so on—what would you do? You answered that you'd either say something to the person about it being wrong or let a manager know.

This is what God asks us to do for one another. If we see our brothers or sisters caught in a sin, we're to restore them gently. That doesn't mean calling them out in front of the church or a group; it's to be a one-on-one conversation. But that's where we miss the mark time and again.

If we do this and do it often, we won't be tearing others down; we'll be building each other up in Christ, and that's what we're called to do. But there's a right way and a wrong way to do this; we can't bash others into the ground about how they're doing everything wrong and not doing anything right—that's not gentle.

How would you want someone to correct you? Passionately but gently, right? And don't worry about being rejected or what others will think of you because remember 2 Timothy 3:16 (NIV): "All Scripture is God-breathed and is useful for teaching, rebuking, correcting and training in righteousness." Also, be open when you're in the wrong because there may be someone watching who may address it with you. And remember that all these conversations are out of and in love.

This part on accountability starts with you. You have to hold yourself accountable first and foremost, and when the time comes, you have to have the courage and boldness to help your brothers and sisters in Christ. We're called to do this together; Proverbs 27:17 (NIV) tells us, "As iron sharpens iron, so one person sharpens another." We have to keep each other in check. And James 5:16 (NIV) tells us, "Confess your sins to each other and pray for each other so that you may be healed. The earnest prayer of a righteous person has great power and produces wonderful results."

Find a person or a group with whom you can meet with regularly to discuss what you never wanted to talk about. Take off your mask and be real with those people. Wouldn't it be better if God heard more than just you praying for your issues? And you'll trust that they're there for you and want you to overcome your burdens because they're carrying burdens too.

Lack of Accountability

Lack of accountability is one of the greatest problem

we face in today's world. It starts small, but it grows into a lifestyle. It can be anything that breaks one of our laws, morals, etc., from rolling through a stop sign to cheating on a spouse to changing your time card. All things start small, but then they snowball. You develop the mind-set of, *Hey, I got away with this the last time. I bet I can do it again and no one will notice.*

You rolled through a stop sign. It is what it is. You didn't come to a complete stop, look both ways, and then proceed; you rolled through it because an officer wasn't there to watch you break the law. If one had been there, you'd have done it perfectly. Same with cheating on your spouse or changing your time card. You do it once and don't get caught, so you do it again even though it's morally wrong and you know you shouldn't be doing it.

Running from accountability is what we humans are good at and have been doing since the beginning of time. But the thing we don't realize is that once this life is done, regardless if God was in our lives or not, He'll hold us accountable.

> So why do you condemn another believer? Why do you look down on another believer? Remember, we will all stand before the judgment seat of God. For the Scriptures say, "'As surely as I live,' says the LORD, 'every knee will bend to me, and

every tongue will declare allegiance to God.'" Yes, each of us will give a personal account to God. (Romans 14:10–12 NLT)

It doesn't matter if you had God in your life or not; He'll judge you and hold you accountable. Look at the mentions of false gods in the Old Testament and how many false gods were created—Baal, Dagon, gold statues created by Nebuchadnezzar, and many more. Why do you think they were created? They had to be created by human being because they were indeed created and given titles and lordship over certain parts of human life. I believe they were created because people were trying to create a sense of falsehood to relieve themselves of being held accountable for their actions and motives. Why else would so many false gods be created? This one was created to justify my passion for lustfulness, and that one was created to justify my passion for death. We could talk about so many of these false gods, but the point is that their creators were trying to escape from being held accountable by God. But God judged them and held them accountable. So we should never take accountability lightly; we have to realize that one day, God will hold us accountable.

Where do you want your accountability to rest when you have to give account for your life—in God almighty or in a false god or idol?

What Does the Bible Say about Correction?

> Two people are better off than one, for they can help each other succeed. If one person falls, the other can reach out and help. But someone who falls alone is in real trouble. Likewise, two people lying close together can keep each other warm. But how can one be warm alone? A person standing alone can be attacked and defeated, but two can stand back-to-back and conquer. Three are even better, for a triple-braided cord is not easily broken. (Ecclesiastes 4:9–12 NLT)

> So encourage each other and build each other up, just as you are already doing. (1 Thessalonians 5:11 NLT)

> And let us not neglect our meeting together, as some people do, but encourage one another, especially now that the day of his return is drawing near. (Hebrews 10:25 NLT)

We don't build each up just to tear each other down. We build each other up so we can be benefits to the kingdom through our good stewardship.

Prayer

Let's end this section on "Correction and Accountability" with a prayer.

Heavenly Father, I want to thank you for the life you have given me and for your Holy Spirit, who flows through me and through my conversations with others. God, I ask you to give me the boldness to have the hard conversations with my brothers and sisters. I ask your Holy Spirit to lead me in all I do. Let everything I do be for you and your kingdom. It's through your Son, Jesus, that I ask these things, amen.

CHAPTER 4

Model

Action Part II

The second action of discipleship is making sure that if we're walking the walk, we're also talking the talk. Nothing says who we are as does the way we act. If we're not the same person Monday through Saturday that we are on Sunday at church, we have a heart issue.

That's how Christians can get the bad rep of being hypocrites, slanderers, and so on and be thought of as worldly Christians because they've compromised between being a follower of Jesus and a follower of the world. We cannot serve two masters; just read Matthew 6:24 about that. We have to be firm in what we believe with no compromise, and we have to do that in a loving way to nonbelievers.

Obeying?

Discipling is not all about teaching the Word; it also involves teaching the importance of obeying Jesus's model. How He lived on earth was perfect, but we're not perfect by any means, and we'll never be perfect all on our own. But we can be perfect through Jesus, the perfect model we should be modeling. In 1 Peter 2:21 (NLT), we read, "For God called you to do good, even if it means suffering, just as Christ suffered for you. He is your example, and you must follow in his steps."

It's another step to grow closer to Him and lead

people to Him at the same time. You know the old saying about actions speaking louder than words; it's true. But we have to remember that the Word—God's Word—speaks louder than do our actions. We have to remember that God's Word trumps everything we do.

When I started wanting to follow Jesus, my mind kept asking, *How can I do this?* Well, I—we—really can't. Not alone. But we can model ourselves after Jesus and be led by the Spirit to be like Him. The hardest part is to just listen to what God is telling us and let the Holy Spirit lead us. For me, letting go was the hardest part because I wanted to be in control. But I've since learned that when we become obedient to what God is calling us to do, all things fall into place.

You won't want to live as you've grown accustomed to. Your sins, whatever those are, have kept you in chains, but you realize the cross has broken those chains and has set you free to live like Christ. When you want to model His perfect example, doing so becomes easier. When your main concern is pleasing God, you won't want to fail Him.

I was so confused about how I could do that and make God pleased with me. Two things about that sentence—God doesn't cause confusion, and I can't do anything without His guidance. If I want to follow the model of Jesus, the Holy Spirit will lead me as to what to say, do, and respond to situations.

If you follow His guidance and obey His command

and will, you won't want to sin. That's not saying you'll never sin again—that will never be the case. But you won't *want* to sin, and when you do, you'll have that feeling of conviction from the Holy Spirit. You'll realize you knew better and should have gotten out of the way and let the Spirit lead you. So when it comes to obedience, the biggest thing is to submit to His will and let the Spirit lead you.

Now remember that everyone sees you in a way that's different from how you see yourself. When you encounter nonbelievers, the only thing they see is you. Who are they seeing? Are you portraying Christ? Do they see Christ in you?

Whom Are We Pleasing?

The way we can be the best Christians we can be—and remember that we're not perfect—is to act as Jesus did. He left an example we can follow. His way is right there in front of us; we just have to take it. But our minds start asking questions: *What will people think of me? What will they say? How will they respond?* Do we want to please people or Jesus? We can't do both, and Jesus should trump people every time.

We should model ourselves after Christ for nonbelievers and believers alike to see. Say there's a young man who has been coming to church for a few weeks and gave his life to the Lord just last week. He sees you at church with your Sunday mask on and watches how you talk to and treat others. Little do you know that he stocks shelves at the grocery store and saw you on Tuesday afternoon talking down to the cashier because something didn't ring up right; you raised your voice and got angry. Is that the person you want this new believer to see? The other you? The one who lives like the world Monday thru Saturday and acts like a saint just on Sunday?

We don't need to make more Christians who don't act like Christ. We have enough of them already, and all they do is give real Christians a bad name. Because we don't know who's watching how we act and talk, we have to bring our A game all the time for Christ's sake.

Creating a Lifestyle

Being a disciple is not something we do when we want to; it's a lifestyle. Luke 9:23 (NIV) says, "Then he said to them all: 'Whoever wants to be my disciple must deny themselves and take up their cross daily and follow me.'" Daily. Not when we feel like it, or when someone is watching us, or once a week, or only at Christmas. Daily. We are to deny ourselves, take up our cross, and model Christ daily. Luke 9:24 (NIV) reads, "For whoever wants to save their life will lose it, but whoever loses their life for me will save it." This doesn't make sense to a nonbeliever and perhaps to a new believer as well. If we want to save our lives, we have to lose them. We can't be selfish in this matter. We give our lives daily to Him so we'll be saved.

Worship

I run across people with an in-the-box view of worship; they think worship occurs only when they're singing praises to God. I'm not saying God doesn't like when we sing praises to Him; He loves that. He also loves it when we commit to Him so completely that our lifestyles change.

Being a disciple is a lifestyle. Worship is a lifestyle. When you model Christ to the best of your abilities, do you think that pleases God? Of course it does! He's seeing a change in your heart that you want to please Him, be with Him, and want to act like Him all the time. What better way is there to show your love of God than to act out His love in everything you do— your lifestyle?

Miserable Worship

It's all about our connection with God, our relationship with Him. How can we continue to live abundantly when we're disconnected from Him? He is the source of life period. Jeremiah talked about this in Jeremiah 2:12–13 (KJV).

Be astonished, O ye heavens, at this, and be horribly afraid, be ye very desolate, saith the Lord. For my people have committed two evils; they have forsaken me the fountain of living waters, and hewed them out cisterns, broken cisterns, that can hold no water.

Here, He was telling us that He was the fountain of living water. When God says it … well, I'm pretty sure it's the truth—just sayin'. But the second part is what I want to talk about here, so let's do some research. A cistern is basically a hole in the ground that was dug to hold water; it was today's version of a storage tank. Once the hole was dug, it was lined with plaster to keep the water in. So Israel had dug its own cisterns, which were cracked or broken. All they had left was an empty hole.

God wants us to be full of His living water, so how can we do this? Well, the better question is how can we do this and be miserable? God wants us to be full of life! How can we worship the God who created everything while we're miserable in ourselves? There's only one answer I can come up with—we're not filled with the living water of God.

And there's only one solution to this problem—to let go of what we've replaced in the spot where God belongs. How can we disciple others and model Christ when we are miserable in our worship? This is the part they can actually see. What do you think runs through their minds when they see us during worship looking like someone just stole our cars? Why would they want to learn about a God who makes us miserable?

Make God first in your life in all aspects and you'll see the biggest change in your life that you'll ever experience. Worship Him for who He is— the God of the universe who wants a relationship with you. What comes in between you and your worship with God? The world today wants to put anything in between you and God.

Forgiveness

Forgiveness is one thing we're all called to do but something we all don't particularly care for. It's just plain hard sometimes. The flesh takes over, and we really just don't want to do it. But we're called to forgive. Matthew 6:15 (NIV) says, "But if you do not forgive others their sins, your Father will not forgive your sins."

I've had a forgiveness issue with some people for a long time. I carried a grudge, anger, and hate issue for a few years. I saw them as I drove by their house or they drove by mine just about every day since they lived in my neighborhood. I thought I had forgiven them in my heart, but every time I saw or even thought about them, I'd be filled with those issues all over. I tried my hardest to put them out of my mind. It was not until I had started to seek the Lord more and more that I felt more and more convicted in how I felt and acted toward them.

I brought the matter up at my accountability meeting; I wanted those I was meeting with to pray for me. I needed guidance and more people praying for me. It was hard in itself to open up and talk about my issues.

I was driving down the road one day and was praying on direction from the Lord—really seeking Him and what His will was for me. The Holy Spirit gave me a conviction like I've never had before. He told me I needed to have a conversation with them. And then He gave me the words to say.

I knew what I had to do and what I needed to say, but I didn't want to do it. I let it stir in me for weeks before anything happened. I let it pass and drove it out of my mind so I didn't have to do it. But at service one day, I knew that day was the day it needed to happen. On my way home from church, I asked the Lord to show me how to say it. He asked me, "How would a servant present this?"

I drove up their driveway. I walked to the front door and knocked and was invited in. They sat, but I got down on my knees, extended my hands palms up—the way I thought a servant would ask for forgiveness—and said, "I'm sorry for the way I acted for the past few years. I acted selfish, and I murdered you in my heart and cast you out. I know that this is not who I am called to be, and I'm here to ask you to forgive me."

I waited for what seemed like an eternity for a response, which really only took a few seconds. *What will they say or think of me?* Then outstretched arms went around my neck and they said, "I've always loved you." The Holy Spirit flowed through the room—chains were broken, and a relationship was restored.

I tell you this personal story about me because it's part of my testimony. I have learned that being obedient to the Holy Spirit and following where He leads you will only help build your testimony to share with others. I celebrate a moment when God used my weakness and fear to make me realize He was truly in control. Submission to God in a situation in which I was not comfortable or confident showed me that's where God revealed Himself the most. Don't let the enemy tell you it's okay to hold a grudge or not to forgive someone. It's your—our—duty to show Jesus's love in our lives through everyone you encounter.

Call It What It Is

The biggest thing for me was my pride. I didn't intentionally try to make people feel less than myself. Most of the time, I never said anything out of line, but all the action was taking place in my mind. I figured that if I never said it, it didn't mean anything, that if it remained in my mind, it didn't hurt anyone. But in fact, I committed it in my heart. And if I committed in my heart, I might as well have said what was on my mind.

> You have heard the commandment that says, "You must not commit adultery." But I say, anyone who even looks at a woman with lust has already committed adultery with her in his heart. (Matthew 5:27–28 NLT)

These verses are the perfect example of how our minds can really deceive us. If I didn't really commit the sin out in the open, it didn't happen, right? On the contrary. When Jesus talked in this verse about the sin of lust, He said basically that if we lusted after someone, we've already committed that sin in our hearts. The same goes for any other sin. All sin is equal and should be treated the same. That's the way God sees it.

Your Kids See Everything

Do you have children? How do you want them to see you? You are the model of their lives. They are moldable; they listen and see everything you do—how you treat yourself, how you treat your spouse, and how you treat them.

When you were growing up, did your parents

influence who you are today? Do you act like them or the complete opposite because you didn't like the way they were? I've heard many people say, "I never want to treat my kids the way I was treated." But too often, I hear, "I've become who my father or mother was." Our heavenly Father has given us the example of how to act and model for everyone to see. Maybe it's time we quit denying who God wants us to be and give up being selfish.

During this transformation in your life, ask yourself, "Whom am I aiming to please with how I act?" Though you want everyone to see Christ in you, your focus needs to be on Christ; pleasing Him is the ultimate goal. If you do this, all the other things will fall into place. You will model the way you talk, act, and treat others on Christ.

Whom Does It Impact?

Have you ever made some decisions based solely on yourself? I have. They were made to benefit me and me alone, and I really didn't care about whom they affected other than me. I know now that those decisions were selfish, prideful, and ignorant and didn't take into account those they were affecting.

One Bible story sticks out in my mind—the story of Daniel and the lions, one of the most popular stories in the Old Testament. Every time I think of that part of Daniel's life, I see it as this long, drawn-out story of him taming the lions, or fighting them, or finding a sword and killing them to save himself. In actuality, the passage is only seven or eight verses long from when king Darius sends him to the lions' den and when Daniel emerges from it.

Every time I read this passage, I see Daniel emerging victorious from the lions' den and I move on. Until recently, when I read it from the king's perspective. He knew Daniel, and he knew his beliefs because by that time, Daniel was pretty high up in rank with the king. The king trusted Daniel and thought highly of him. When the officials came to the king to issue the decree about no one praying to any god or idol other than the king, the king being, well, the king, decided it was a great idea since it would make him better than everyone else. He made the decree with only himself in mind. He didn't care whom else this decree might impact. That was until the officials told him that Daniel had broken his decree.

Darius was very upset that Daniel had been caught, and he tried to get him out of the dilemma. But he was forced to keep his word about anyone who broke the decree being thrown into the lions' den even if it was someone he thought highly of. When Darius ordered Daniel to the lions' den, he told Daniel that Daniel's God would get him out of this somehow.

Once Darius placed his seal on the stone slab, he

went home. He couldn't eat. He couldn't sleep. I'm sure at that point that Darius had no clue what he would have to put Daniel through when he made that decree. He was sad and most likely angry at himself for letting this happen in the first place.

The next morning, he ran, not walked, to the den out of concern for his friend. Once he found out that Daniel was safe, he was happy, so happy that he put those who had opposed Daniel and their families all in the lions' den.

In Daniel 6, Darius showed us what could happen when we make decisions that involve only ourselves, how a prideful decision could impact those we care about. This is why it's so important to follow the Holy Spirit when making decisions; He will not lead us anywhere but down God's path.

Tithing Is a Model?

We need to model other things for Christ, things that no one but the Lord sees. Tithing is one. When you break it down, tithing translates to "first tenth." What that means is the first part of the top line is God's. What got me was when I would figure my bills and divvy out what goes where, I'd pay everyone else first and give God what was left. I've been convicted by the Holy Spirit over this time and again. Look at it this way—it's all God's anyway, so are we going to give Him back what's already His? "The master said, 'Well done, my good and faithful servant. You have been faithful in handling this small amount, so now I will give you many more responsibilities. Let's celebrate together!" (Matthew 25:23 NLT).

We sometimes ask God, "Why haven't I been given more?" I believe that we hold ourselves back more that we think. What usually comes between us and our relationship with God is ourselves. I believe the parable of the talents relates strictly to that question. The servant was faithful over little and was ruler over many things. The part that I get out of this teaching is that if God can't trust us with money, why would He trust us with souls? If we handle our affairs the way He wants us to handle them, He will give us much more. So are we giving control of our finances to the Lord or keeping that for ourselves and forgoing what we could be given?

First Things First

God is a jealous God. Deuteronomy 4:24 (NIV) tells us, "For the LORD your God is a consuming fire, a jealous God." He wants to be first in everything. Our finances are always a touchy topic because they're so personal. We don't go around bragging about how much we make, but we do go out and complain about it. It's a hard thing to do when our budgets are not used to it, but it will work. God will bless us for giving back to Him.

But God doesn't want just the first tenth of your finances; He wants to be first with your time too. He wants your time in the morning, not after you've worked a full day and worked out in the gym after that and are too exhausted to give Him anything. At that point, you can't focus on Him. That's why He wants your time first thing in the morning when your mind is fresh and you can be more in tune with Him.

In the morning, I read the Bible, do my devotions, and spend time with the Lord; He is then on my mind for the rest of the day. Look at it this way—if you put the armor of God on in the mornings before anything, you've prepared yourself for the day. If you put it on at night after the battle, what good does that do you? Probably not a whole lot.

What Does the Bible Say about Modeling?

> Whoever claims to live in him must live as Jesus did. (1 John 2:6 NIV)

> And you should imitate me, just as I imitate Christ. (1 Corinthians 11:1 NLT)

> My old self has been crucified with Christ. It is no longer I who live, but Christ lives

in me. So I live in this earthly body by trusting in the Son of God, who loved me and gave himself for me. (Galatians 2:20 NLT)

So God created man in his own image, in the image of God he created them; male and female he created them. (Genesis 1:27 NIV)

We were created in His image; we were created to model Him since the beginning. We fail daily—we have to recognize that—but we also have to recognize that we are redeemed through Christ and that we can do His work and lead people to Christ through Him alone, not us.

Prayer

Let's end this section on "Model" with a prayer.

God, Thank you for sending your Son, Jesus, to this world to be the perfect model for us. It is only by and through Him that we can live like Him. I ask that you give me the strength every day to strive to act just as He did. Let your will be done in my life so I can be your vessel to better your kingdom. I thank you for what you have shown me as I strive to be like your Son and model His perfect life. Thank you for your amazing love that you give me. In Jesus's name, amen.

CHAPTER 5

Love

We can do all these things well though not perfectly, but if we are not doing them for the right reasons, they won't work. When we decide to follow Jesus and mimic His life, we have made a life-altering decision. Philippians 1:21 (NIV) reads, "For to me, to live is Christ and to die is gain."

I must surrender myself daily to the Lord. The only reason that will work for all of these things is because I'm in love with Jesus. I want to show how my relationship with Him is my reason for being here, and I want to share it. If I don't do it for and with His love, it won't work.

Why Love?

Love is the reason we have salvation, which is freely given to all. John 3:16 (NIV) reads, "For God so loved the world that he gave his one and only Son, that whoever believes in him shall not perish but have eternal life." I'm pretty sure that verse describes how much He loves us. If anyone has a question about His love for us, this verse should answer it.

Like many of you, I am a parent, and I'd do anything in my power to not have anything happen to my son. When I say anything, that means everything. But yet in our sin, God sent His only Son. Freely. For me and you. We will never be able to measure the extent of His love for us.

Why would God send His only Son as a living sacrifice for all humankind? We have sinned from the beginning and will be sinners on the last day. We have committed every sin under the sun.

How Much Love?

We claim to follow and know Jesus but still fail Him daily. We don't deserve Him. We should all be cast into the flame but—and there's always a but—"God demonstrates his own love for us in this: While we were still sinners, Christ died for us" (Romans 5:8 NIV).

God's love for us outweighs our sin every time. Because of what Jesus did for us on the cross, He truly bore all sin. He died for whatever sins were committed five minutes, five days, five years, or any time after He died on the cross.

Our minds can't fathom the amount of God's love for us; it's a never-ending supply in our never-ending sin. It's always one more than what we have. If I've sinned one thousand times, He has me covered at a thousand and one. You get the picture. Whatever we have done, He's got us covered.

The Greatest

Jesus told us how to follow the law in His answer to a question about the Commandments. When asked by experts on the law about which was the greatest commandment, Jesus gave everything summed up in two commandments.

> "Teacher, which is the most important commandment in the law of Moses?" Jesus replied, "You must love the LORD your God with all your heart, all your soul, and all your mind. This is the first and greatest commandment. A second is equally important: Love your neighbor as yourself. The entire law and all the demands of the prophets are based on these two commandments." (Matthew 22:36–40 NLT)

If we love God with all we are and love our neighbor as ourselves, we can come as close to fulfilling the law as we can. Discipling allows for no difference in the way we love people.

Think of the most influential spiritual people in your life. How do you think you would have turned out if they hadn't sown the seed of Christ in you? Would you have turned out as you did? Whoever sowed that first seed in you loved you enough to invest in you.

How many blessings are we falling short on receiving because we haven't loved as we have been commanded to love? How many people are not going to enter the kingdom because we didn't show them love? It's our calling to love one another. Let's not let any more of His people down by not loving them.

Cultural Love

Based on the way this world is, I believe we've forgotten as a generation what Christ's love looks like—it's pure agape love, and it's freely given.

I see the way that our culture is today, and I don't like it. I see so many Christians giving into worldly cultures and beliefs, and that shouldn't be happening. Our love for God and His Word should be our immovable foundation. Compromise is not an option here. Jesus said,

> If the world hates you, remember that it hated me first. The world would love you as one of its own if you belonged to it, but you are no longer part of the world. I chose you to come out of the world, so it hates you. Do you remember what I told you? "A slave is not greater than the master." Since they persecuted me, naturally they will persecute you. And if they had listened to me, they would listen to you. They will do all this to you because of me, for they have rejected the one who sent

me. They would not be guilty if I had not come and spoken to them. But now they have no excuse for their sin. Anyone who hates me also hates my Father. If I hadn't done such miraculous signs among them that no one else could do, they would not be guilty. But as it is, they have seen everything I did, yet they still hate me and my Father. This fulfills what is written in their Scriptures: "They hated me without cause. But I will send you the Advocate— the Spirit of truth. He will come to you from the Father and will testify all about me." (John 15:18–26 NLT)

We can't be of the world and of God; it's one or the other—we're either politically or biblically correct.

What's Your Passion?

If you're passionate about a certain topic, that can drive you to do something about it. For example, I'm pretty passionate about discipleship, so I wrote this book about how we all can be better disciples to others in need, and I'll put it into action. It is a great honor to be able to be a vessel for the Lord by doing His work; I'm trying to make a difference.

Some people may have big hearts for homeless people

but talk about homelessness only when the subject comes up in conversation or when they're sharing a post or ranting about it on social media. They want to make other people see what they can do to help the homeless while they're posting pictures of really expensive meals with their families the cost of which could have fed a homeless person for a month.

If we love something and are passionate about it, we should do something about it. We shouldn't wait for the next person to make a difference. The Lord has put a calling on our lives that we shouldn't ignore. It's time we start doing what we're called to do instead of just talking about it.

Tough Love

Growing up, I heard my parents and grandparents say, "I did that out of love." Back then, I couldn't see how spankings, groundings, or any other form of punishment could have come from any love. I felt anger, disappointment, and rage. If that's what love was, I didn't want anything to do with it.

But over the years, I learned lessons from and grew closer to my parents and grandparents from their discipline. I became a father myself and saw the difference. Some types of punishment are prompted by anger and such, and now I see that nothing good comes from that. But punishment meted out in love is real tough love. Why did I punish you? Because you deliberately disobeyed me. It's a form of protection almost. I don't want to see you get hurt physically or emotionally. I've been through that before; I know what the outcome is, and I don't want you to experience that.

Our heavenly Father is concerned for our well-being just as we are for our children's well-being. Sometimes, we have to learn the hard way, and most of the time, it's when we try to go against God's will or direction. The Holy Spirit is there to let us know we've gone astray or have done something we shouldn't have. That's the feeling of conviction we get. And it's the same when we need to hold each other accountable as Christians.

Right Reasons

"I want to be in this for the right reason." That's a line from a song my band sings. We want to grow our relationship with the Lord, but we must do that for the right reasons. If I'm learning, I'm truly trying to learn about God and His character. I want to learn how to love Him more by reading His Word. If I am teaching, I am truly trying to grow the kingdom of God. I teach others about His agenda, not mine.

If I am correcting my brother or sister in Christ, I am truly doing it as a gentle command from the Lord and not out of hate, anger, or jealousy. I am doing it out of love to help keep someone on the right track. If I am modeling, I am modeling the image of Christ so He will be seen through me as His vessel, not for any other agenda. His will alone; my selfishness gets left behind.

Discipleship is a must to strengthen the kingdom of God, but we have to be patient; it's not a quick fix or an overnight process. It takes time—weeks, months, years—however long it takes. Let's learn, teach, correct, model, and love the world in the name of Jesus. It's the only way to truly change the world.

Let Go

I've visited many churches, became a member of a few, and served in leadership positions in a couple of them. I've found that there's always something that changes all the time—the people. Sometimes, problems arose because of anger or because someone made someone upset. But we don't have time to get into that here. We'll focus on why people leave for the good. And that's not that "Good! They're gone" type of good either. It's for the good of the kingdom. They are being called to pursue their ministries to benefit the kingdom.

We have to be okay with their leaving. Training disciples doesn't mean we expect certain people to stay in the same place for all their lives. Yes, some people are called to stay in positions for a long time, but others are called to be in certain positions for a couple of weeks. But the thing is that we have to let them follow where

God is leading them. Let's look at Paul and Barnabas for an example.

> After some time Paul said to Barnabas, "Let's go back and visit each city where we previously preached the word of the Lord, to see how the new believers are doing." Barnabas agreed and wanted to take along John Mark. But Paul disagreed strongly, since John Mark had deserted them in Pamphylia and had not continued with them in their work. Their disagreement was so sharp that they separated. Barnabas took John Mark with him and sailed for Cyprus. (Acts 15:36–39 NLT)

Though Paul and Barnabas disagreed about John Mark going with them or not, that's not the point I'm trying to make. Paul was being led to go one way, and Barnabas was being led to go another. If they had gone against the Spirit leading them, the outcome would have been completely different. They needed to separate; they needed to be apart and start different ministries. They could then reach more people, train more disciples, and plant more churches than if they had stayed together. What better way to spread the gospel worldwide than to create more traveling training groups.

So when we have friends or family who need to

branch out and do what the Spirit is calling them to do, we shouldn't hinder their walks or their callings to fulfill what we want them to fulfill. Jesus didn't call us to be disciples in one place; He called us to be disciples all over the world.

What Does the Bible Say about Love?

> Love does no wrong to others, so love fulfills the requirements of God's law. (Romans 13:10 NLT)

> Love is patient, love is kind. It does not envy, it does not boast, it is not proud. It does not dishonor others, it is not self-seeking, it is not easily angered, it keeps no record of wrongs. Love does not delight in evil but rejoices with the truth. It always protects, always trusts, always hopes, always perseveres. Love never fails. But where there are prophecies, they will cease; where there are tongues, they will be stilled; where there is knowledge, it will pass away. (1 Corinthians 13:4–8 NIV)

> Be completely humble and gentle; be patient, bearing with one another in love. (Ephesians 4:2 NIV)

Dear friends, let us love one another, for love comes from God. Everyone who loves has been born of God and knows God. (1 John 4:7 NIV)

Hatred stirs up conflict, but love covers over all wrongs. (Proverbs 10:12 NIV)

This is how we know what love is: Jesus Christ laid down his life for us. And we ought to lay down our lives for our brothers and sisters. If anyone has material possessions and sees a brother or sister in need but has no pity on them, how can the love of God be in that person? Dear children, let us not love with words or speech but with actions and in truth. (1 John 3:16–18 NIV)

Prayer

Let's end this section on "Love" with a prayer.

God, the love you show us is more than we can imagine. The love it took to send your only Son to the cross to bear the world's sins is great—beyond compare.

Give me the heart and mind to love as you love. I want to live just as your Son did and love as He loved.

Let your love flow through me to all the people I meet so they may experience you. Let them see your love and your character. It's only by your Son, Jesus, that I ask these things, amen.

CHAPTER 6

What's the Next Step?

Romans 8 talks a lot about being in the flesh—"weakened by the flesh" and "living according to the flesh." Let's read the first few verses together.

So now there is no condemnation for those who belong to Christ Jesus. And because you belong to him, the power of the life-giving Spirit has freed you from the power of sin that leads to death. The law of Moses was unable to save us because of the weakness of our sinful nature. So God did what the law could not do. He sent his own Son in a body like the bodies we sinners have. And in that body God declared an end to sin's control over us by giving his Son as a sacrifice for our sins. He did this so that the just requirement of the law would be fully satisfied for us, who no longer follow our sinful nature but instead follow the Spirit.

Those who are dominated by the sinful nature think about sinful things, but those who are controlled by the Holy Spirit think about things that please the Spirit. So letting your sinful nature control your mind leads to death. But letting the Spirit control your mind leads to life and peace.

For the sinful nature is always hostile to God. It never did obey God's laws, and it never will. That's why those who are still under the control of their sinful nature can never please God. (Romans 8:1–8 NLT)

Flesh

I heard the best and simplest way to describe what the word *flesh* means. Take away the *h* and reverse the other letters and you end up with the word *self.*

Living in the flesh is all about me, I, my, mine, we, our, us. Are we being led by the Spirit or by the flesh? We cannot grow the kingdom of God by working in the flesh; it has to be by the Holy Spirit. Paul wrote,

But you are not controlled by your sinful nature. You are controlled by the Spirit if you have the Spirit of God living in you. (And remember that those who do not have the Spirit of Christ living in them do not belong to him at all.) (Romans 8:9 NLT)

He didn't beat around the bush; he called it what it was. Either you have it or you don't.

Will You Take the Next Step?

So what's the next step? Is it time for you to take a seat in the pew, the chair, or the bleachers and let someone else train the next generation of Christians, or is it time for you to fulfill what God has called you to do—make disciples?

God made it clear through His Word what the Great Commission was; Matthew 28:19–20 (NLT) reads,

> Therefore, go and make disciples of all the nations, baptizing them in the name of the Father and the Son and the Holy Spirit. Teach these new disciples to obey all the commands I have given you. And be sure of this: I am with you always, even to the end of the age.

Whom are we here to please? Ourselves and the rest of the world or God almighty?

Prayer

One of the most important things I can do for myself or for anyone else is to pray; prayer is our direct line of contact with our heavenly Father. But at the same time, it's one thing I don't take nearly the advantage of that I need to.

It's easy to just stop and say a prayer, but a lot of people including myself get caught up in the business of the day and prayer slips our minds. As we discussed in the first part of this book about our relationship with God, how would we feel if our spouses treated us dispassionately? The principle is the same here. God wants us to be in constant prayer with Him, but we often fail to communicate with Him even once or twice a day.

If we stopped and realized the power of prayer—man, would that change our lives.

Power of Prayer

You've asked others to pray for you or over you in certain situations in your life. I know that because I've done it many of times and continue to do so. We do that because we know that if someone other than ourselves is praying for us in the same manner we are, God will know how important it is to us because we've stepped out and asked for help in the form of prayer.

This is what Paul and Silas did when they were in jail. At midnight, they were praying and praising God when an incredible earthquake opened the jail doors and unshackled all the prisoners (Acts 16:25–26). They were in need, so what did they do? They prayed and praised God, and look what happened.

That's exactly how God wants us to respond to what

we're going through. God answered prayers then, and He'll do it again today. Just think of the doors that will be opened for us; just think of the chains holding us back that will break.

Pray, Pray, Pray

Be in prayer constantly about whom you will encounter on this new journey you're about to take. Pray to the Holy Spirit to lead you and give you the right words to say. Pray that your heart will be strong in the face of strife and rejection. Pray about being in the Lord's will. Be in prayer about all you do.

Prayer is your direct line to God. He is there and is willing to grant you anything you need. He will guide you; He will never lead you astray or away from Himself.

Go and Make Disciples

The time is now. The Lord has put a calling on all our lives. Why would we want to waste time while people are dying and going to hell? It's harsh, but it's the truth. I don't want to see anyone end up there; I wouldn't wish hell on my worst enemy. It's up to me and you to go out and build up the population of God's kingdom and put up roadblocks to the entrance of hell.

We are called to love everyone, so why would we

receive the greatest gift of all, salvation through Jesus Christ, but not want everyone we know to have that same gift? It should truly be the gift that keeps on giving. So let's change our mind-set about walking with and by the Spirit, throw away our personal agendas, and change the world. Let's be bold in our faith. Let's do what God has called us to do. Let's put aside our selfish pride and tell others about the Lord Jesus Christ.

I'm calling you out to take this to heart as I have and go out and make disciples.

Assimilation

This section may not be what you are called to do, but it's something that needs to be in place in your church to benefit new believers and the body of Christ.

I think assimilation is one of the parts lacking in the discipleship process. I did not even hear of this process for believers until recently. I was having lunch with my pastor one day and telling him with a heavy heart what I was being called to do. I told him I wanted to help people find where they belonged, to build relationships with them, and use the gift of discernment to help point them in the right direction. I was being led to this ministry though I had no clue where to start.

He said, "What you told me is the process of assimilation."

"What's that?" I asked. I'd never heard of that.

He told me it was exactly what I had just described to him.

I asked, "Where do I go from here to start this process?"

It went from there to teaching part of our Growth Track classes—discovering purpose and making a difference. This process should be in every Christian teaching and discipleship ministry. So let's start with what assimilation means—absorbing groups of different cultures into the main cultural body.

How does that relate to discipleship? I'm glad you asked. When you get new believers, how do you determine where they belong? Do they know that right off the bat, or do they need guidance to help them figure it out? The process of assimilation involves helping new believers—groups of different cultures—find their places in the body of Christ—the main cultural body.

If you break it down to simple terms, and I mean very simple terms, discipleship is helping believers plant their roots in good soil so their foundations in Christ will be secure. Assimilation is helping believers find out where in the body of Christ they belong.

This is where I've seen the church fail time and again. It does a good job of reaching unbelievers, but then it almost immediately it retreats. "It's too much work to disciple and assimilate new believers." That's the mind-set we have to break. We can no longer sit back and watch all the new believers who have come to Christ fall away from their relationships or watch them become stagnant relationships in which they don't know where to go.

This is a process just like discipleship; I believe they go hand in hand. Once new believers have their roots planted firmly in Christ, they need to learn where their places are in the body of Christ. Discipleship is so important because it teaches them how to get to know God—who He is and what His character looks like, what He expects of them, what His vision is for their lives, and what their gifts are. But what's all that if they don't know where their places are in the body? It means they will have knowledge but have no way to apply it. And no application means no action.

> What good is it, dear brothers and sisters, if you say you have faith but don't show it by your actions? Can that kind of faith save anyone? Suppose you see a brother or sister who has no food or clothing, and you say, "Good-bye and have a good day; stay warm and eat well"—but then you don't give that person any food or clothing. What good does that do? So you see, faith by itself isn't enough. Unless it produces good deeds, it is dead and useless. (James 2:14–17 NLT)

James was not saying that good deeds get you to heaven or that the lack of work will keep you from getting to heaven. What he was saying was that by faith, we will be changed or transformed and that the lack of works results in an unchanged life or having spiritually dead hearts.

This is the result of having knowledge but not putting it into action. What kind of service are we giving our fellow brothers and sisters in Christ by dumping them after they get saved because helping them past that point would take up too much of our time? What if those who were our spiritual influences had left us on the side of the road during our journeys? Would we be where we are today?

Jesus called us to serve one another on our journeys. Will we help serve them on their journeys, or will we retreat? The decision is ours.

About the Author

Brett Harig is a common guy out of Statesville, North Carolina. Multi-Tasker is the best way to describe him. Being a husband, father, business owner, musician and now a writer on top of all that keeps him occupied. Growing is his passion for discipleship and the call to write this book.

To connect with Brett please visit:
Facebook.com/asyourgoing;
on Instagram @Asyouregoing
or email at asyouregoing@gmail.com

Printed in the United States
By Bookmasters

Printed in the United States
By Bookmasters